Contents

1	Sikhism	1
2	Guru Nanak	4
3	Neither Hindu nor Muslim	9
4	Teaching and singing	14
5	Guru Arjan and the Adi Granth	20
6	Guru Gobind Singh and the Khalsa	25
7	The Guru Granth Sahib	32
8	Gurdwaras	37
9	Birth, marriage and death	43
10	Festivals	49
11	The Sikhs today	53
	Word list	58
	Useful addresses	60
	Index	61

Sikh Belief and Practice

M R Thompson

Series Editor Jan Thompson

Edward Arnold

© M R Thompson 1985

First published in Great Britain 1985 by
Edward Arnold (Publishers) Ltd
41 Bedford Square
London WC1B 3DQ

Edward Arnold (Australia) Pty Ltd
80 Waverley Road
Caulfield East
Victoria 3145
Australia

British Library Cataloguing in Publication Data
Thompson, M.R.
    Sikh belief and practice.
    1. Sikhism
    I. Title
    294.6   BL2018
ISBN 0-7131-7362-9

The Publishers would like to thank the following for their permission to
reproduce copyright illustrations: David Richardson: pp 11, 15t, 33t,
55; Government of India Tourist Office: p 23; John Twinning: p 30;
Dr Mel Thompson: p 39; Nick Hedges: p 45; Popperfoto: p 51.

The publishers also wish to thank Macmillan Publishing Company for
permission to use an extract from Noss: *Man's Religions* and Routledge
and Kegan Paul plc for an extract from Cole and Sambhi: *The Sikhs:
their Beliefs and Practices.*

Set in IBM 10 point Press Roman by ⋔Tek-Art, Croydon, Surrey.
Printed in Great Britain by The Bath Press, Avon

Preface

This book continues a series on world religions for pupils of 14 years and over. Requiring no previous knowledge on the part of the reader, it gives a detailed summary of the Sikh religion and sets this against the geographical and cultural context in which it arose. Alongside factual details about the development of the Sikh community and its religious practices are explanations of Sikh beliefs and attitudes, to encourage a deeper understanding of this religion. The book does not attempt to give a comprehensive survey of the historical developments, but outlines those facts which are needed in order to explain the significance of religious and ethical attitudes.

The Sikh religion is numerically small by world standards, and is closely associated with the culture of the Punjab. Nevertheless, its blending of Indian ideas with those of monotheism, and its devotional and ethical simplicity, make it an easier religion to study than Hinduism, for the pupil not already familiar with Indian thought. The universal human questions are touched on in the text, and the 'Issues to discuss' section at the end of each chapter gives scope for pupils to reflect further upon them. Rich in symbolism of dress and ritual, Sikhism presents a vivid, wide-ranging contribution to a course on world religions.

1 Sikhism

In the north of India, between the desert and the Himalayas, lies the land of the Punjab (see Fig. 2). The name 'Punjab' means 'land of the five rivers'. The rivers Sutlej, Beas, Ravi, Chenab and Jehlam are all tributaries of the Indus, flowing southwards through Pakistan towards the Arabian Sea.

It is a part of the world which has experienced much religious conflict. To the south and east lies India, with the Hindu religion and culture; to the west lie the Muslim countries of Pakistan, Afghanistan and Iran (see Fig. 1). The Punjab, in its culture and its geography, is the land where these two great religions have struggled together.

The Sikh religion sprang from the life and vision of one man, Nanak, who lived in the 15th century C.E. (Common Era, the equivalent of A.D.). He sought peace by going beyond the divisions between the Hindu and Muslim faiths. He was the first of ten human *gurus* (or teachers) whose followers are known as Sikhs. The word 'sikh' means 'follower' or 'disciple'.

One hundred and fifty years ago there was an independent Sikh kingdom in the Punjab, ruled by Maharaja Ranjit Singh; now the land is divided between India and Pakistan. On the Indian side of the border, with its religious centre at Amritsar, is the homeland of the greater part of the 15 million followers of the Sikh religion.

To those of you who know something of Hinduism and Islam, Sikhism may seem to have a curious mixture of ideas from those religions. Like Hinduism, for example, there is belief in reincarnation; and yet there is no caste system. Like Islam, there is only one God and no images are used in worship; and yet there is no heaven or hell, and no veiling of women. But Sikhism is not a conscious attempt to combine the other faiths. Rather, Guru Nanak saw the need to reform Hinduism (possibly influenced by some Muslim ideas, as well as those of other Hindu reformers), and then go beyond both Hinduism and Islam. Soon Sikhism was to become a distinct and unique form of religion, with definite beliefs and rules for living; although Sikhs have continued to believe that other religions can be good if they are practised with inward sincerity.

Although the majority of Sikhs still live in the Punjab, there are Sikh communities in many other countries. In Britain there are about half a

1

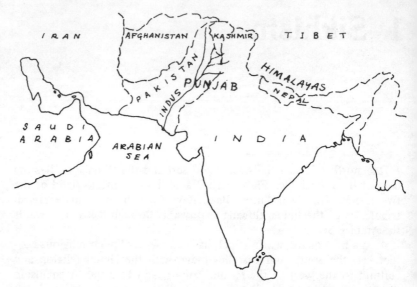

Fig. 1   The Punjab — divided between Pakistan in the West and India in the East.

Fig. 2   The Punjab, Notice that the places where Nanak was born and died (Talwandi and Kartarpur) are now in Pakistan, not in the Indian state of Punjab.

million Sikhs. The men are recognised by their beards and turbans, and the women may wear the traditional Punjabi dress of *shalwar* (loose-fitting trousers) and *kameeze* (the tunic or dress worn over them) with a chiffon scarf, called a *dupatta* or *chunni*, thrown over the shoulder. Their religion teaches them to be a hard-working and hospitable people, willing always to share their beliefs with others. Although the majority of Sikhs are of Indian origin, it is possible for any person to become a Sikh if he or she is prepared to accept the teaching of the *gurus*, as set down in the Sikh scriptures, the *Guru Granth Sahib*.

In the chapters that follow we shall see that Sikhism is a simple religion, requiring devotion rather than intellectual effort or elaborate ritual; and one which rejects rigid beliefs on the grounds that man can never fully know God, and that all religions can display some elements of truth.

We shall also see that it is a religion which requires of its followers serious commitment and a high moral standard. In seeking to bring about peace and to oppose injustice, it has a double-edged sword as part of its emblem, and a history of warfare and martyrdom.

This book is concerned with the Sikh religion and those who practise it. Other people may call themselves Sikhs, and may even wear traditional Punjabi dress, although they are not religious. For them it is simply a way of indicating that they come from the Punjab and from a Sikh family.

Make sure you know
1 the name of the land from which Sikhism arose
2 the name of its founder
3 the names of the other two main religions in that area

See if you understand
4 why the geographical position of the Punjab is so important for understanding the Sikh religion

Issues to discuss
5 Can all religions point towards the same truth?
6 Do you think it is a good idea for immigrants to keep the customs (e.g. dress, food and language) of the country from which they come?

2 Guru Nanak

Guru Nanak was born on April 15th 1469 in the village of Talwandi, about forty miles west of Lahore, in what is now Pakistan (see Fig. 2). In his honour, the village is now called Nankana Sahib. His father was a Hindu, an accountant and farmer. The family was well respected and, as members of the second highest caste (*Kshatriya*), they could study the Hindu scriptures, called the Vedas; but they could not preach from them, a privilege reserved for the highest (*Brahmin*) caste.

Nanak was therefore brought up in a Hindu family and studied that religion. He also came to understand Islam, for since the 11th century that part of India had been ruled by Muslims, and the Punjab was part of the great Mughal empire. Even the local ruler of his village, a man called Rai Bular, had been converted to Islam and encouraged attempts to reconcile the two religions.

The only information we have about the life of Nanak comes from four collections of stories about him called the *Janam Sakhis*. The literal translation of this is 'birth evidences', for they try to show evidence of divine inspiration from Nanak's birth onwards. The earliest recorded *Janam Sakhis* come from the early 17th century, many years after Nanak's death, and their historical value is questioned by many scholars. One of them, the *Bala Janam Sakhi*, is traditionally thought to have been dictated by Nanak's close friend Bala, in the presence of his successor, Guru Angad. Bala often appears in pictures of Guru Nanak.

According to these stories, Nanak was too fond of meditating to keep his mind on his work as a youth, and was not interested in being a herdsman. Stories record that even when young he was critical of formal religion. He refused to accept the sacred thread to denote his status as an adult member of his caste, saying that it was powerless to influence a person's behaviour, good or bad. He also infuriated his Brahmin teacher by asking why it should be necessary to be a Hindu at all. Why should it not be enough simply to be a man?

Eventually, his brother-in-law managed to secure him a government job in Sultanpur, and there he settled with his wife Sulakhani and had two sons, Sri Chand and Lakhmi Das. During these years at home with his family, his religious search continued, and he was joined by a Muslim friend and musician from his home village, called Mardana, who was to remain his companion for most of his life.

What kind of religion did he practise? All our evidence is influenced by the later practice of Sikh worship, but it seems that his approach was similar to that of the *Sant* tradition in Hinduism. This was a reforming movement in Hinduism, and it combined two themes:

(1) that man's salvation comes through the practice of *Bhakti*, or devotion, involving singing, praise and the repetition of the name of the god being worshipped.

(2) the *Nath* tradition, which used *hatha yoga* (disciplined exercise of the body) and insisted that religion should be a matter of interior discipline, and had no need of external rituals or images.

The *Sant* tradition used the common language of the people for worship, dispensed with the need for priestly rituals, and emphasised the need for personal devotion.

One of these Hindu reformers, whose hymns appear in the Sikh scriptures, is Kabir, and it is possible (but not certain) that he and Nanak knew one another. Kabir wanted to express a unity beneath the many gods of Hinduism, and a simplicity in worship. He claimed that the love of God could free *anyone* (of whatever caste) from the *Law of Karma*, by which the soul is bound by its good or bad actions to continue through a succession of rebirths. Once free of *karma*, the soul could be absorbed back into the Absolute through love.

Nanak refused to accept the idea that God might be found especially in some image, and found particular religious actions and rules quite unnecessary. God was present everywhere, and within each human heart. All that was necessary was personal devotion to God, and the living of a moral life. All people were therefore equal, no matter what their caste; and devotion to God went beyond the division between Hindu and Muslim. Religious ceremonial was therefore little more than a distraction: it was the inner spiritual life that mattered. Here is some advice that he gave to Muslims:

Let compassion be thy mosque,
Let faith be thy prayer mat,
Let honest living be thy Koran,
Let modesty be the rules of observance,
Let piety be the faith thou keepest;
In such wise strive to be a Muslim;
Right conduct the Ka'aba; Truth the Prophet,
Good deeds thy prayer,
Submission to the Lord's Will thy rosary;
Nanak, if this thou do, the Lord will be thy protector.
(Noss – *Man's Religions* page 238)

Notice that he does not say that all these things are bad in themselves. He implies that they are good *only* if they are made to express an inner attitude.

5

Fig. 3   Guru Nanak: his hand is raised in blessing and in it he holds a mala, like a string of beads but made of cotton, which is used as an aid to meditation.

Nanak was a reformer of religion. He pointed beyond particular actions, and beyond religious divisions. In doing this he started a religious tradition which was soon to take on a special character of its own. Because of this, Sikhs claim that their religion is unique, although it shares ideas with both Islam and Hinduism.

Nanak became the first *guru* of the Sikh religion. *'Guru'* means 'teacher'. Sikhs believe that God himself is the true *guru* (*Sat guru*), but that he makes himself known through earthly messengers who are also known as *gurus*. Therefore Guru Nanak, the other nine human *gurus*, and the Sikh scriptures (the *Guru Granth Sahib*) are given great respect. The faith which they teach is called *Gurmat*, which is literally 'the *guru's* teaching'.

Sikhs can divide people into two categories. *Gurmukh* is the term for a person through whom the *guru's* (i.e. God's) voice is heard, and *Manmukh* describes a person who only reveals his own mind and his own self-interest.

Inspired by a vision (which we shall consider in the next chapter), Guru Nanak left his family and started to preach and wander about, both among Hindus in India, and among Muslims, travelling (according to tradition) as far as Mecca, the very centre of the Islamic faith. He took with him Mardana, who accompanied Nanak's religious hymns on a simple stringed instrument called a *Rebec*.

In 1521 Guru Nanak settled with his family and disciples at Kartarpur. The earliest description of this stage in his life comes from the writings of Bhai Gurdas (1538-1637) a poet who organised the gathering together of the scriptures under Guru Arjan (see Chapter 5).

He organised a communal farm, and set up a routine of manual work with prayer and the communal singing of hymns. He made the settlement a place of hospitality, establishing the Sikh tradition of the communal kitchen, called the *Langar*. In doing this, he established the twin features of every Sikh community, *Sangat* and *Pangat*. *Sangat* means 'association', the gathering together of worshippers in a single community. *Pangat* means being in a row, and refers to the custom of sitting side by side to eat in the communal kitchen without any distinction being made between castes. Only those who are able to sit and eat with one another as equals in the *pangat* can therefore become members of the *sangat*.

Make sure you know
1 when Guru Nanak was born
2 from what Hindu caste he came
3 the name of the musician who accompanied him

See if you understand
4 why Sikhs claim that their religion is unique
5 what is meant by *'guru'* and why the term is used both of certain people and of God

7

Issues to discuss

6 The young Nanak was not always successful at work. Is it possible to be highly religious and also useful in practical work?
7 Nanak asked why he should be a Hindu and not simply a man. Is it possible to be religious without belonging to a religion?

3 Neither Hindu nor Muslim

Married at the age of nineteen, and with two sons, Nanak lived a settled life at Sultanpur and seemed to have satisfied his employers as a store keeper in charge of the state granary. In spite of some complaints, his business management and accounts were said to be faultless when checked.

Although deeply religious, Nanak did not seek the path of an ascetic — leaving home and family to achieve some personal spiritual goal. Rather, he thought it important to work and take on domestic responsibilities. Even towards the end of his life, at Kartarpur, his community was not like a monastery, for his followers lived and worked within their families. This set the pattern for the whole Sikh *Panth* (meaning 'community' or 'people'). Sikhs regard honest business and hard work as a basic duty, and see the married state and family life as the norm.

When he was about thirty, Nanak had an experience which marked the start of a new period in his life. Like many Hindus, it was his custom to take an early morning bathe, and he did so in the local river, called the Bein. One morning he disappeared. His companion, who had been waiting on the bank with his clothes, feared that he had drowned and raised the alarm. The river was dragged but the search yielded no body. Then, after three days, Nanak returned home, having had a vision, he said, of being in God's court and receiving a cup of nectar to drink. In one of his hymns he described the experience like this:

I was a minstrel out of work,
The Lord gave me employment.
The mighty one instructed me,
'Night and day sing my praise'.

The Lord summoned the minstrel
To his High Court.
On me he bestowed the robe of honouring
him and singing his praises.

On me he bestowed the Nectar in a cup.
The nectar of his true and holy name.
Those who at the bidding of the Guru

9

Feast and take their fill of the Lord's holiness
Attain peace and joy.
Your minstrel spreads your glory
By singing your word.
Nanak, through adoring the truth
We attain to the all-highest.

(*Adi Granth*)

These verses show both the content of Nanak's proclamation (praise of God who is able to give man peace and joy) and also the form in which he was to deliver it, through songs and poetry.

At first he was reluctant to say anything about his experience. He joined a group of holy men, without seeming to conform to either the Hindu or the Muslim path of religious discipline. On being questioned about this he said:

There is neither Hindu nor Mussulman (Muslim) so whose path shall I follow? I shall follow God's path. God is neither Hindu nor Mussulman and the path which I follow is God's.

Clearly, what Nanak experienced took him beyond such differences. He set out on his mission of preaching and teaching, dressed in a rather bizarre way to illustrate his message. He wore the usual Hindu lower garment (the *dhoti*) and sandals, and over it he put a mango-coloured jacket and a white sheet. His hat was the sort worn by Muslim holy men, and yet he had the saffron mark on his forehead, like a Hindu. Round his neck he had a necklace of bones, which he used as an aid to prayer, rather as Catholics today use the rosary. In such garb he would be recognised as neither a Hindu nor a Muslim.

In his teaching he (like some other Hindu reformers) criticised some features of Hinduism, but he also rejected some Muslim practices. For example, from Hinduism

— he rejected the use of images
— he rejected the authority of the Vedas and the Brahmin priests
— he saw no need for severe discipline nor the giving up of wordly business and family life
— he rejected ritual washing
— but most importantly, he rejected the caste system. All Sikhs were to be equal and were to eat together (*Pangat*).

and from Islam

— he rejected food regulations. Unlike Hindus, Sikhs can eat meat, but it should *not* be prepared in the special ritual way (Hallal) that is required by Muslims. Many Sikhs think that it is better to be vegetarian.
— he rejected the veiling of women

10

Fig. 4   Pangat. Eating together is a sign of equality and fellowship. Men and women sit separately in rows, and food is brought round to them, set out on individual trays. All gurdwaras have a communal kitchen, and these meals are shared after worship on all main festivals and other special occasions.

11

- he rejected the need for special postures in prayer, or the necessity of facing Mecca
- he rejected the finality of Muhammad as a prophet

In all this he was concerned to show that it was the interior, personal attitude that counted, rather than the external action. Once, on seeing Hindus in the river at Hardwar throwing (or pouring out) water eastwards, towards the rising sun, as an offering to their ancestors, Nanak started throwing water in the opposite direction, saying that his fields near Lahore needed watering.

Yet this experience of the vision of the cup of nectar was not a negative one, although as a result of it he could point to the limitations of other religions. It was a positive experience of the presence of God, and under its influence he is said to have uttered the *Mool Mantra*. This means the 'perfect' or 'basic' mantra: a short statement of belief with which the Sikh scriptures open, and which can sometimes be seen written up on the canopy which goes over the copy of the scriptures in the Sikh temple, or *gurdwara*.

There is but one God whose name is True, the Creator,
devoid of fear and enmity, immortal, unborn, self-existent,
great and bountiful.
The True One was in the beginning, the True One was in the
primal age.
The True One is, was, O Nanak, and the True One also shall be.

It may sound as though this experience was the moment at which Nanak became 'enlightened', realising truths that he had not understood before. But Sikhs do not believe this. They claim that Nanak was already enlightened from birth, and that this vision was simply the sign that he should start his mission.

The reason for this belief is connected with the idea of reincarnation, a belief that Sikhs share with Hindus. According to this, the good or bad deeds that a person performs in this life will determine what his or her next life will be. This continuous succession of births and deaths is determined by the *Law of Karma*, and it is something from which a person hopes eventually to be released — something which Nanak claimed could happen to any person through love. Once a person has become spiritually at one with God, *Moksha* (or 'release') is achieved, and there is no need for further rebirths.

Now Sikhs believe that Nanak's was an example of a rare *'non-karmic'* birth. He had already become at one with God and did not need to be born again, doing so simply in order to be able to carry out his mission for the benefit of others. The stories in the *Janam Sakhis* therefore describe a special kind of radiance in his face as a child, the recognition of his importance by an astrologer at his birth, and claim that he spoke on spiritual matters at the age of five. He knew everything, but waited for this special moment before making his mission public.

Sikhs believe that there have been a number of such messengers, and alongside the ten *gurus* of their own religion, they include such men as the Buddha, Muhammad, Moses and Jesus. God remains the true and unique *guru*, but his word is communicated through his chosen messengers.

Make sure you know
1 the name of the opening of the Sikh scriptures
2 the main features of Islam and Hinduism that Nanak criticised

See if you understand
3 what Nanak meant by saying that there was neither Hindu nor Muslim
4 the meaning of *non-karmic* birth

Issues to discuss
5 Nanak rejected the caste system. Is it possible to have a society that is completely rid of class divisions?
6 Nanak deliberately chose a form of dress that would confuse and provoke those who saw him. How important is it to conform to (or rebel against) what society expects you to wear?

4 Teaching and singing

For the next twenty years or so, Nanak, accompanied by Mardana, was to travel far afield on missions (called *udasis*), teaching and singing. Traditions, gathered in the *Janam Sakhis*, describe their visits to places of religious importance for both Hindus and Muslims.

Sometimes he would use an action to explain a religious point. According to the *Puratan Janam Sakhi*, Nanak went to Mecca. There he was found, at the time of evening prayer, asleep with his feet pointing towards the Ka'aba, the central shrine of Islam which worshippers face when they pray. This was considered a sign of disrespect. When he was awakened and challenged, he asked simply for his feet to be pointed towards any point where God was *not* to be found. For him, no one place was any more or less holy than any other, since God was present everywhere.

Mostly, Nanak taught through his poetry, which Mardana set to music. These hymns were easily memorised by his followers, and form the basis of the Sikh scriptures. The religion is not therefore presented in the form of a logical argument, or a set of beliefs, but in a series of devotional songs.

From these we find two central beliefs upon which the teachings of Nanak are based:

1 There is one God. As set out in the *Mool Mantra* (see Chapter 3), God has no form, no beginning and no end. He is beyond man's understanding, and cannot be described. Yet Nanak claimed that he could be experienced and known personally. He is personally concerned with all creatures, and lives *within* them. This was a theme that he shared with many of the Hindu reformers of his day. It is expressed in the Sikh scriptures in many ways: this one comes from a passage by a later *guru* (Guru Tegh Bahadur).

> Why do you go to the forest to find God? He lives in all and yet remains distinct. He dwells in you as well, as fragrance resides in a flower or the reflection in a mirror. God abides in everything. See him, therefore, in your own heart.
>
> (*Adi Granth*)

Fig. 5 Music plays a major part in Sikh worship. The traditional instruments used to accompany the singing are harmoniums and drums. Here musicians are sitting in the front of a gurdwara.

Fig. 6 Nanak sits with Mardana, the musician on his right, and his helper Bala on his left. Bala waves a chauri to fan the guru, regarded as a sign of great respect.

15

Although Hindus call their gods by various names, Nanak held that God was beyond names. To show this, he is sometimes called *Nam*, which means 'name', or *Sat Nam*, 'True Name'. He may also be called *Sat Guru*, 'True teacher'. God is beyond time (*akal*) and beyond names (*anami*); there is no single word for God in Sikhism, and no definition of him.

2   Men are by nature wilfully blind to the truth about God. They may sense that they are in need of the salvation offered by religion, but tend to think that this need can be satisfied by performing religious exercises at a temple or mosque. Yet these external actions, Nanak claimed, only served to keep man in his state of blindness, or illusion. The Indian word for this human illusion is *maya*. In some forms of Hinduism, *maya* can be taken to mean that the world itself is an illusion. This is not so in Sikhism. For Sikhs it is the values by which people live and the hopes which motivate them that are *maya*. The world itself is real.

Maya is reinforced by five impulses which chain people to this world. They are: lust; anger; greed; attachment to worldly things; pride. To live dominated by these impulses ensures that a person will continue in the cycle of death and rebirth, and prevents that person from achieving *mukti*, or 'release' into the presence of God.

Guru Nanak believed that man's effort could never be enough to free him from these evil impulses. A person needed devotion, inspired by God, in order to be able to live a life of practical goodness. Only through God's love could human evil be overcome.

Man's salvation, and the escape from the illusions which dominate his life, comes through the *sabad* (word) which he learns from his *guru* (teacher). The idea of *sabad* is not limited to written or spoken words. Anything which enables a person to glimpse something of God is *sabad*, and whatever communicates that insight is the *guru*. Therefore a human being, like Guru Nanak, will be called 'guru' simply because he is a person through whom the follower has glimpsed something of God; and, of course, God himself remains the true *guru*, or *Sat Guru*. Naturally enough, the hymns of the Sikh scriptures, because they express the insights of that religion, are also called *sabads*.

What is seen in these glimpses of God? Sikhs claim that it is *hukam*, which means 'order'. There is a basic order in the universe, and once you have perceived it, you are able to live more at one with it, in a state of natural harmony. It is through *maya* that we normally fail to see this order; once this is overcome, unity with God is achieved.

If there is order, then why is there suffering in the world? To this most basic religious question, the Sikh answer takes two forms:

1   Suffering may be the result of self-centredness. We want everything in the world arranged to suit ourselves, and are disappointed when it is not so.

16

2   Suffering may be an opportunity for a person's action to be turned into something good e.g. persecution may lead to martyrdom, and such suffering is a witness to the truth. This can therefore become part of a person's service to his or her fellow men. A person may also be required to suffer in the struggle against evil.

Devotion, Guru Nanak taught, was simple and did not depend upon the elaborate rituals of the Hindu tradition. Following the *sant* tradition of devotion in Hinduism, the Sikh is to repeat the name of God, *Nam*.

As well as this simple use of *Nam*, repeated over and over, Nanak encouraged the singing of devotional hymns. He did this by composing them in the common language (Punjabi) rather than in the traditional sacred language of the Hindus, *sanskrit*. For the first time, the common low-caste people could meditate upon and understand the meaning of hymns. Previously they would not have been allowed access to the scriptures, and would not have understood *sanskrit*.

The best known of his religious poetry, now incorporated into the *Guru Granth Sahib*, and coming at the very beginning of the scriptures to indicate its importance, is the *Japji*. This is composed of 38 stanzas (called *pauris*) and a concluding section. The *pauris* literally mean 'steps': so the *Japji* is seen as a ladder of ideas, taking the reader up through the whole of Nanak's vision of reality, step by step through the important questions of the religious life.

It is always preceded by the *Mool Mantra* (see Chapter 3) and takes about twenty-five minutes to recite − a task faithful Sikhs perform every morning. It is the only part of the scriptures not to be set to music. This is probably because Indian music is set in different moods, corresponding to different times of the day, and this tends to limit the traditional use of any one particular hymn. The *Japji*, however, is considered suitable for any time of day.

The first of the *pauris* states that no amount of thinking, nor even silent meditation, can make God known, for he is quite beyond the mind of man. Man's task (as explained in *pauri* 2) is to seek out God's will, which is described as the force that shapes and determines everything that happens in the world. There is little room in Sikh thought for man's freedom to change the world: everything is determined. If some are great and others are small, that is all part of God's will, and you must accept people as they are.

For a person to think that he or she can actually possess or control life is *maya*, illusion. God's name (*Nam*) is the substance out of which everything comes, and we are just a tiny part of it − we come from God and will return to him.

This then leads to a description of the sort of devotion which is appropriate:

Naught is our own; all is His that we possess, this life and
  all is His!
With what offerings, could we enter His Temple?
With what virtue, His Presence?
What words have we on our lips to win His Delight?
Meditate on His *Nam* at Morn, wet with the ambrosia of the
  day-break!

(from pauri 4)

By tradition therefore, the Sikh will meditate upon *Nam* and recite the
Japji in the morning. But this is not expected to bring about some
external revelation. Rather, knowledge comes from within oneself,
illuminating the outside world, taking the worshipper beyond the
illusions of life. The same *pauri* continues:

> The Dawn of Divine Knowledge comes from within, and man sees
> God as the Light Revealing.

Guru Nanak says that there may be worlds beyond our known world,
and that man is quite unable to comprehend the scale of the universe.
He does not need to give an explanation of the world in order to have
faith. Nor, since God is in everything, does he need the idea of miracles
as special moments when God acts. Indeed, the whole idea of God
changing the natural order of the world goes against the awareness of
hukam. More than that; for a person to crave for special signs and
miracles only shows that he or she is still bound to *maya* and lacks
faith. This allows the Sikh faith to be compatible with all scientific
theories, for none conflict with its idea of God.

Man is therefore to be devoted to God without asking questions
about Him:

> Ours is to lose ourselves in worship and adoration, nor need we ask,
>   Why?
> No need to fathom the Unfathomable: As the rivers flow to the sea
>   with their song, let us flow on to the Infinite, not knowing how
>   wide is the ocean's flood.
> Like an ocean is the Lord Almighty.
> If one has wealth-heaps as high as pyramids,
> Let him be ever so rich, yet is he less than the little ant, the ant that
>   forgets not its Maker.
> (The small man that enshrines the Sultan within is all-great.)

(pauri 23)

Love is more important than wealth, and just as gold is refined in a
furnace so, in the closing *pauri* of the Japji, man is said to be made pure
through love.

18

Make sure you know
1 the meaning of the words *'sabad'* and *'hukam'*
2 the name of the language of the Sikh scriptures
3 the name of the religious poem at the beginning of the scriptures

See if you understand
4 the meaning of *maya* in Sikhism
5 the Sikh explanation of suffering

Issues to discuss
6 The Sikh religion emphasises the importance of devotion rather than intellectual understanding. Which is more important in religion, the mind or the heart?
7 'The Conquest of the World is but the Conquest of thy Self' (from *pauri* 28/9). What do you think this means?

5 Guru Arjan and the Adi Granth

Before Nanak died, he chose a disciple called Lehna (who proved to be more faithful and obedient than the Guru's own sons) to be his successor, and renamed him Angad, which means 'my limb'. He said that his spirit would be in Angad's body, and placed five coins and a coconut at his feet as a sign of transferring his authority. The coconut is said to represent the world, and the five coins are the five elements: air, earth, fire, water and ether (once thought to be an invisible medium filling the spaces between particles). The coins were also designed and made by man, and so they could represent the handing over into the care of the new Guru all the world of man as well as the world of nature.

There were altogether ten *gurus*:

1	Guru Nanak	(1469-1539)
2	Guru Angad	(1539-1552)
3	Guru Amar Das	(1552-1574)
4	Guru Ram Das	(1574-1581)
5	Guru Arjan	(1581-1606)
6	Guru Hargobind	(1606-1644)
7	Guru Har Rai	(1644-1661)
8	Guru Har Krishan	(1661-1664)
9	Guru Tegh Bahadur	(1664-1675)
10	Guru Gobind Singh	(1675-1708)

In character and age the *gurus* differ widely from one another. Guru Amar Das was already an old man of seventy-three before he took office, and Guru Har Krishan a child of five. Yet Sikhs believe that they all preached the same message. Two of the *gurus*, Arjan and Gobind Singh, stand out as being of particular importance for the shaping of the Sikh religion as we know it today.

Since the start of his preaching, the hymns of Guru Nanak would have been remembered and passed on among his followers. Guru Angad devised and developed a form of script for them, for previously there does not seem to have been any written form of the Punjabi language. This script is called *Gurmukhi* (literally 'the *guru's* script') and is used to this day in Sikh worship and as the official language and script of the Punjab. During the time of Guru Amar Das there was a collection of the hymns, but it was Guru Arjan who first brought together and authorised the Sikh scriptures, called the *Adi Granth* ('first writings' — first, that is, in the sense of being of prime importance).

Guru Nanak himself composed 976 hymns and to these Guru Arjan, who was a poet and philosopher, added 2,216 verses of his own as well as hymns by the earlier *gurus*. It was customary for poets to include their names in the last line of their poems. All of the *gurus* use the name Nanak in their poetry, and in order to distinguish between one and the other the word *Mahala* and a number appears with each piece of writing. *Mahala* 1 stands for Guru Nanak, *Mahala* 2 for Guru Angad, *Mahala* 3 for Guru Amar Das and so on. It emphasises the belief that all the *gurus* shared the same insight and the same message.

The collection of hymns was taken down, according to tradition, by Bhai Gurdas (who was himself a poet) in 1603 and 1604. The original manuscript is still in existence and is held by the Sodhi family at Kartarpur in Jullunder province (*not* the Kartarpur founded by Nanak).

A most remarkable thing about this collection is that it contains the work of non-Sikhs as well as Sikhs. Most prominent among the non-Sikhs is Kabir, who has 541 hymns included. His thought is close to that of Guru Nanak. In one of the hymns (on page 1,136 of the *Adi Granth*) he says:

I am neither Hindu nor Muslim.
(The One) *Allah-Ram* is the breath of my body.

In Chapter 3 we saw that Guru Nanak said the same thing. Kabir here uses a Hindu (*Ram*) and Muslim (*Allah*) term for God, and joins them.

The hymns are called *sabads*, and out of a total of 5,894, no fewer than 938 are by non-Sikhs. This is an expression of the openness of the Sikh religion, not claiming a monopoly of truth.

Between an opening (which contains the *Mool Mantra*, the *Japji* and 14 hymns that are repeated elsewhere) and an epilogue of assorted pieces, the hymns are divided up into 31 sections, each of which is set to a particular tune (*rag*). Within each section the arrangement is the same. First come hymns by the *gurus* in order from Guru Nanak to Guru Tegh Bahadur (the ninth *guru*, whose hymns were added later by Guru Gobind Singh), then comes Kabir, the Muslim Sheikh Farid, Namdev, Ravidas and other poets.

Written in the *Gurmukhi* script, the *Adi Granth* is always printed on 1,430 pages, so that each page in each edition is identical. It contains no stories but only devotional poetry, set to music. Yet this poetry, and the beliefs contained within it, are regarded as so important for the Sikh community that tradition says that Guru Arjan himself bowed before it, showing that it represented The Truth.

Guru Ram Das had founded a city (named, after him, Ramdaspur) on land that, according to one tradition, was given to his wife as a present from the Emperor Akbar. There he constructed a pool, called the 'Pool of Immortality'. It quickly established itself as the centre of the Sikh religion, and became the city of *Amritsar*, which means 'Pool of Nectar'. There, in the middle of the pool, Guru Arjan was to build the *Harimandir* (House of God) or *Darbar Sahib* (the Lord's Court). It is better known now as The Golden Temple since much of it is covered in gold leaf, after being extensively rebuilt in the 19th century.

The building of the Harimandir started in 1598. Its foundation stone was laid by a Muslim holy man called Mian Mir — another indication of the openness of Sikhism. In 1604 both it and the *Adi Granth* were completed, and the scriptures were installed there, in what is now the best known of all Sikh *gurdwaras*, or temples.

The Harimandir has doors on all four sides, as a sign that the Sikh religion is open to people of all castes. It is also necessary to go *down* steps as you enter it. This is to remind the worshipper that every person must go down in humility when preparing for a meeting with God.

It is joined to the side of the lake by a bridge, and across this every morning, heralded by trumpets, is carried the copy of the *Adi Granth* from where it has been guarded during the night. Many Sikhs visit Amritsar, crossing the bridge and filing round the copy of the *Adi Granth* installed there, although they are under no religious obligation to do so. There is no pilgrimage (in the literal sense) in Sikhism. Guru Nanak claimed that the true pilgrimage was the inner spiritual journey.

Amritsar was on the trade route between the Middle East and India, and quickly became a flourishing commercial city. Under Guru Arjan the Sikh religion too was strengthened, and for a time was accepted by the Mughal authorities. The Emperor Akbar was interested in religion and philosophy. He read the *Adi Granth*, finding nothing subversive or dangerous in it, and even visited Guru Arjan at Amritsar.

Guru Arjan's success was, in part, responsible for his death. The following year (1605), Emperor Akbar died and was succeeded by Jahangir, who resented the religious and commercial popularity of Amritsar. He resolved that Guru Arjan should be converted to Islam or be killed. He was arrested and tortured. Finally, on May 30th 1606, he was killed. One tradition says that he was roasted alive, another that he was killed in the River Ravi at Lahore, from which his body was never recovered. The martyrdom of Guru Arjan is commemorated by Sikhs every year.

Before he died, Guru Arjan gave instructions to his son, Guru Hargobind, which were to influence the direction in which the Sikh community was to go. He told him to sit fully armed upon his throne and to maintain an army.

Guru Hargobind was imprisoned at Gwalior for some time, but after his release was able to organise an army which had some success during a time of persecution under the Mughals. Then, in 1634, he retired with many of the Sikh community to the Shivalik Hills, which lie

Fig. 7   The Golden Temple at Amritsar. It is the most important
centre for the Sikh community, and receives many visitors each year
from all over the world. In 1984 the buildings surrounding the lake
were the scene of fighting between Sikh nationalists and the Indian
army.

between the plains of the Punjab and the Himalayas. He, and the *gurus* who followed him, spent most of their time there.

The Shivalik Hills, as the name suggests, have a special association with the worship of the Hindu god Shiva, a god who balances life and death, creation and destruction. It was an area dominated at that time by the *Sakti* culture, which glorified militarism, and saw the sword as a symbol to be respected. Also, from this time, the Sikh *Panth* (or people) became increasingly influenced by the *Jats*, a rural peasant caste. Although castes ceased to exist within the Sikh *Panth*, the caste from which Sikhs came had an influence on the community. The *Jats* were naturally more warlike in their thinking than the *Kshatriya* caste of business men and officials from which Guru Nanak and many other early Sikhs had come.

The sword (as we shall see later) was to become a prominent symbol in the Sikh religion, and the idea of military discipline goes well with the commitments and responsibilities taken on by the adult Sikh. It does not seem to have been found in the writings of Guru Nanak or the three following *gurus*, but was forced upon the Sikhs during the years of persecution under the Mughals, and has been reinforced and taken into the spirit of the religion through a history of almost continuous conflict.

For a time then, Amritsar declined in importance for Sikhs, and the tenth Guru, Gobind Singh, never visited the city. In the 18th century, it became the central meeting point of separate Sikh groups, but Maharaja Ranjit Singh, the famous ruler of the independent Sikh kingdom chose Lahore rather than Amritsar as his capital. Nevertheless, later in the 19th century its importance grew, and now it is once again the centre of the Sikh religion.

Make sure you know

1 who authorised the Sikh scriptures (*Adi Granth*)
2 the name of the city which became the centre of the Sikh religion
3 the usual name for the temple that stands in the lake there

See if you understand

4 why hymns by non-Sikhs are included in the *Adi Granth*
5 why Sikhs became more militant under Guru Hargobind

Issues to discuss

6 Sikhs believe that there is good to be found in all religions if they are followed sincerely. Is it ever worth dying, therefore, rather than being converted?

24

6 Guru Gobind Singh and the Khalsa

During the time of Guru Har Rai (1644-1661) and Guru Har Krishan — a child of five when he became *guru* only to live another three years (1661-1664), there had been peace for the Sikh community. Yet towards the end of the rule of the ninth *guru*, Tegh Bahadur (1664-1675), there came further conflict with the Mughal rulers.

The *guru* was approached by some Hindus from the Kashmir. They complained that Aurangzeb, the Emperor of Delhi, had been forcing conversion to Islam upon them. He agreed to help them, but because of this was charged with sedition and heresy and ordered to appear before the Emperor in Delhi. After presenting his case, Guru Tegh Bahadur was threatened with death if he himself did not accept Islam. He insisted on the freedom to follow his own religion, and was therefore beheaded. He was not the only one to suffer. His friend Bhai Diala was boiled alive in a cauldron of water, and another follower, Bhai Mati Das, was killed by being sawn in two. The bodies of these martyrs were then displayed on the gates at Delhi.

With the death of his father, Gobind Singh became *guru* in 1675. All around him the Hindus were complaining. They were not allowed to hold government posts, or to ride horses, and they had to pay a special tax. Many of them joined the Sikhs at this time, seeing in their community the only hope of opposition to the Muslim rulers.

Guru Gobind Singh realised that, in order for it to survive, the Sikh community needed two things:

(1) The Sikhs had to become a committed and disciplined army.
(2) All caste differences between those of Hindu origin had to be set aside, so that those from the lower castes could be encouraged to take a full and equal part in their new religion.

He achieved these two objectives in a dramatic way when the Sikh community gathered to celebrate the festival of *Baisakhi* in April 1699. He initiated the first Sikhs into an organisation called the *Khalsa* (meaning 'the pure') and in doing so he gave to the Sikh religion its most distinctive features.

Before a large crowd whom he had called together during the festival of *Baisakhi* at Anandpur, Guru Gobind Singh took out his sword and called for a Sikh to come forward who was prepared to give his life for the faith. After some time a volunteer came forward and was taken into a tent, from which the *guru* emerged with his sword covered in blood. Then he asked for another volunteer. The crowd became anxious, and some started to leave. Eventually five volunteers were taken into the tent. Guru Gobind Singh then came out with the five men alive. Some scholars suggest that the blood was that of a goat, but traditional Sikh belief holds that the five men were actually killed and then raised from the dead. They are called the *Panj Piaras*, which means 'the five beloved ones'.

He then called for others to come forward and commit their lives to the defence of the Sikh faith and the struggle against oppression. Once the commitment to lay down their lives did not appear quite so literal or so immediate, the five were joined by thousands of others.

He then performed a ceremony of baptism, called *Amrit Sanskar*, which admitted the volunteers into the new community of the *Khalsa*. The same action is used today to show that a Sikh is ready and willing to be fully committed to the faith and prepared to take on its responsibilities.

Sugar was dissolved in water to make a sweet drink called *amrit*. This he sprinkled over the volunteers and also gave it to them to drink. This sweet drink represents immortality, (notice that the lake, around which the city of *Amrit*sar was built, was called the Lake of Immortality). The act of drinking it represents taking God into oneself, and therefore being beyond the power of death.

Not all Sikhs, in 1699 or the present day, are baptised in this way. Those who would not be prepared to fight for their faith, or who find all such rituals unnecessary, are called *Sahaj Dhari* and may still be regarded as true believers, as long as they accept the teachings of the *gurus*. Those who accept *Amrit* are called *Kesh Dhari Singh*. They are given a new name at baptism — *Singh* for men (meaning 'lion') and *Kaur* for women (meaning 'princess'), and they are to regard themselves as warriors under discipline.

For the *Khalsa*, Guru Gobind Singh prescribed five symbols, usually called 'the five 'K's'.

1 **Kachha** (shorts) Those who need to be agile and ready to fight cannot wear a long garment, like the *dhoti* worn by Hindu holy men. Members of the *Khalsa* therefore wear shorts, as a sign that they are always ready to defend their faith. Today, some regard ordinary long trousers as *kachha*, others consider underpants as *kachha*, although the shorts worn by those who observe the tradition strictly are of a special design. The main idea is discipline and readiness. As a modest form of dress, *kachha* also represent sexual discipline and control.

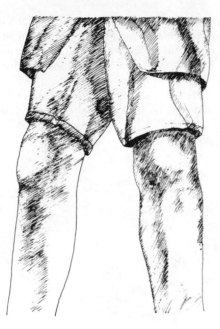

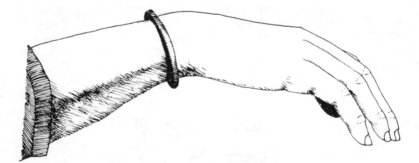

2 Kara (bangle) This is a steel bangle worn on the right wrist. It may be taken to represent restraint and indebtedness to the *gurus*' teaching. The fact that it is a circle makes it also a symbol of eternity and of unity. It is a reminder of the oneness of God and of the Sikh community. The circle is used as a symbol for God on the Sikh flag.

27

3   Kirpan   (sword) This expresses power and freedom. It has a practical purpose, for defence, and also a spiritual meaning. The member of the *Khalsa* is a spiritual warrior, fighting against the five evil tendencies in human nature (see Chapter 4). Today the *kirpan* often takes the form of a brooch, or an emblem set into the side of the comb with which the Sikh will fix his hair. Sikhs in Britain are allowed to carry a *kirpan*, as long as it does not become an offensive weapon.

4   Kesh   (hair) Sikhs of the *Khalsa* do not cut their hair. Following the tradition of many holy men, it becomes a sign of dedication. Men have their hair bunched up and fixed with a comb, or tied in a knot. The hair is then bound up within the turban, which is customary but not one of the requirements of the *Amrit* ceremony. A turban may be worn by any Sikh old enough to tie it himself, without waiting for baptism.

5 Kangha (comb) This is necessary to keep the hair clean, and therefore becomes a natural symbol for physical and spiritual cleanliness. (On a practical level, the Sikh also has a rule that hair should be washed every four days.) The *kangha* pins the hair under the turban, and may have the symbolic *kirpan* set in it.

With these five symbols, the Sikh becomes a member of the 'Brotherhood of the Pure', the *Khalsa*, and carries on his or her person at all times these reminders of the religious commitments made at baptism.

The usual age for being admitted to the *Khalsa* is about 16 to 18 years, and it is not generally allowed before the age of 14. The ceremony takes place before five Sikhs, called the *Amrit Dhari*, who represent the original volunteers of 1699. While portions of the scriptures, prayers and the poems of Guru Gobind Singh are being read out, these five kneel round a bowl in which the sugar water is to be mixed. They kneel forward, with right knees on the ground and left knees raised. Touching the bowl with their left hands, they take it in turn to stir the mixture with the *khanda*, a double-edged sword. (Those of you who know some Yoga may recognise this posture: it is known as 'The Warrior'.)

The sugar water (*amrit*) is sprinkled over each initiate's eyes, hair and hands five times. Each time, the person being baptised has to say '*Waheguru ji ka Khalsa*' (The *Khalsa* is chosen of God) and '*Waheguru ji ki fateh*' (Victory is God's).

This ceremony is taken very seriously. Before it takes place, the rules are read out. These involve:

(1) wearing the five 'K's
(2) accepting the teachings of the ten human *gurus* and of the *Guru Granth Sahib*
(3) accepting responsibility for all others within the Sikh brotherhood
(4) abstaining from adultery, and from taking tobacco or alcohol
(5) working honestly and giving 10% to charity
(6) not practising magic or using charms
(7) being ready to sacrifice everything for the faith

29

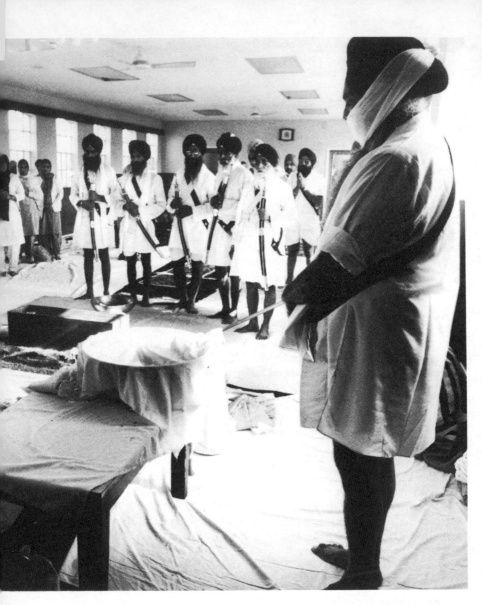

Fig. 8   Amrit Sanskar: the service of baptism into the Khalsa. Here the amrit is being prepared in a bowl. Notice the five Sikhs with their long kirpans who stand ready to take part in the ceremony. They represent the five men originally baptised by Guru Gobind Singh.

If any of these rules is broken, it is possible for a Sikh to do penance, and even to be re-baptised.

Guru Gobind Singh was a poet as well as a military man. He knew Persian and Sanskrit as well as Punjabi, and wrote poetry in all three languages. His poems were gathered together after his death in a book of 1,428 pages, called the *Dasam Granth*. It is difficult to read, although some passages are popular. Some of the poems reflect the new military emphasis that he brought to Sikhism:

> The purpose for which I am born is
> To spread true religion and to destroy evil doers, root and branch.
> Blessed are those who keep God in their hearts,
> And sword in their hands to fight for a noble cause.
> When there is no other course open to man,
> It is but righteous to unsheath the sword.

Many who had been lower caste Hindus found in the *Khalsa* a new self-respect, and this was a time when many rural peasants (called *Jats*) became Sikhs. The status of the *Khalsa* was immediately recognised, and today many would regard it as the only true way to follow the Sikh religion fully. In the definition of the Sikh religion called the *Rehat Maryada*, drawn up in 1945, every Sikh must believe in the necessity of *amrit*. Those groups who do not accept it (see Chapter 11) are regarded as very much on the fringe of Sikhism.

On the military front things went badly for Guru Gobind Singh and the *Khalsa*. Of his four sons, two were killed in the battle of Chamkaur, and the other two were captured and bricked up alive in a wall at Sirhind. Eventually, after some time as a fugitive, Gobind Singh himself was stabbed to death in 1708.

Revenge was soon to come. Before his death, Gobind Singh appointed Banda Singh as his military commander, and he, within the next eight years, reversed the military defeats. The town of Sirhind was razed to the ground.

Make sure you know
1 the name of the *guru* who founded the *Khalsa*
2 the five 'K's

See if you understand
3 why the sword is used as a symbol of the Sikh faith
4 why the *Khalsa* may be regarded as the start of Sikhism as we know it today

Issues to discuss
5 Is it right to defend oneself or to kill in the name of religion?
6 Does a true Sikh need the five symbols of the *Khalsa*?

7 The Guru Granth Sahib

Sikh tradition records that, before he died, Guru Gobind Singh placed a coconut and five coins on a copy of the *Adi Granth*, and declared that there would be no more human *gurus*. In future the Sikh community was to seek its inspiration and guidance from the scriptures. These he had completed by adding hymns by his father to the collection already authorised by Guru Arjan. From that point on, the *Adi Granth* was termed and treated as a *guru*, and was to be known as the *Guru Granth Sahib*. *Sahib* is a term meaning 'master' or 'lord', and with '*Sri*' (another term of respect, almost like the English 'Sir') the full title of the scriptures becomes *Adi Sri Guru Granth Sahib*.

The handover of power from the human *guru* to the scriptures was not quite as straightforward as it may seem, however; for there existed another principle, called the *Guru Panth*. This declared that the local congregation of Sikhs (the '*Panth*' or 'People'), when they came together to make a decision on a matter to do with their religion, had the authority of a *guru*, and could decide things on his behalf. This was the case even during the lifetime of Guru Gobind Singh, and after his death, it existed as an authority alongside that of the *Guru Granth Sahib*.

Today however, the *Guru Granth Sahib* is the unchallenged authority on all matters of Sikh belief and life. Interpretation of the scriptures is done by the *granthi* week by week in each *gurdwara*. In cases where the community has some dispute about its meaning, the matter can be referred to the most senior places of study and interpretation for the Sikh religion. Chief of these is the *Akal Takht* in Amritsar. There are four such *Takhts*, the others being at the *gurdwara* at Patna Sahib (birthplace of Guru Gobind Singh), the Keshgar *gurdwara* at Anandpur (where the *Khalsa* was started) and the Hazur Sahib, Nanded (where Guru Gobind Singh died). The *granthis* of these four seats of authority, along with the *granthi* of the Golden Temple at Amritsar, may be required to meet and make a decision on matters of special importance.

The great respect given to the *Guru Granth Sahib* is shown by the way in which it is treated in a *gurdwara*. In the Golden Temple at Amritsar it is read continuously in low chant, while visitors file round it as a sign of respect and devotion. When it is carried over the bridge from the treasury each morning, it is held high in a silver casket. Sikhs bow before it (as did Guru Arjan) and make offerings. It is most impor-

Fig. 9   The Adi Sri Guru Granth Sahib. It is always printed in exactly the same way, with the same number of pages, and is always treated with great respect.

ੴ ਸਤਿਨਾਮੁ ਕਰਤਾ ਪੁਰਖੁਨਿ ਰਭ ਉਨਿਰਵੈਰ

ਅਕਾਲ ਮੁਰਤਿ ਅਜੂਨੀ ਸੈਭੰ ਗੁਰ ਪ੍ਰਸਾਦਿ ॥

Fig. 10   This is the Mool Mantra in Gurmukhi script. The first two characters mean 'God is One' — ik oankar (see below p 38).

tant to realise, however, that the *Guru Granth Sahib* is *not* being worshipped. The Sikh believes that God himself (*Sat Nam*: the True Name) is to be worshipped, whereas the *gurus*, including now the *Guru Granth Sahib*, are to be treated with respect, as being the vehicle through which the will of God is made known.

To own a copy of the scriptures is a great responsibility, since a room in the house has to be set aside for it — just as would have been the case if one were accepting one of the human *gurus* as a guest. Many Sikhs do not have a copy because they cannot afford to offer it this degree of respect. They may hope to own a large enough house for there to be a spare room to be used as a *gurdwara* (although the term *gurdwara* is most commonly used for a public temple, it also applies to *any* place which houses a copy of the scriptures). Sikhs learn sections of the scriptures by heart, and some families will have a *gutka*, which is a selection of passages from the *Adi Granth*, along with some extracts from the *Dasam Granth* and the prayer *Ardas*.

In private as well as in public, the *Guru Granth Sahib* is the centre of Sikh worship. By tradition (following the advice in the fourth *pauri*) Sikhs rise early and recite the 38 *pauris* of the *Japji*, followed by the common prayer of Sikhs, called the *Ardas*. Other prayers may follow, and at night before going to sleep they may recite the Sohila, or evening hymn of Guru Nanak (from page 12 of the *Guru Granth Sahib*). During the day, a Sikh may visit a public or private *gurdwara* for *darsan*, or 'audience'. The worshipper enters the room, bows low before the *Guru Granth Sahib* and makes an offering. He or she may then accept a little *Karah Parshad* (see Chapter 8) from the *granthi* in charge of the scriptures. It is an opportunity for quiet, to seek guidance and inspiration.

Sometimes a cotton rosary, called a *mala*, of 108 knots is used. This form of prayer is called *Nam Simran* (calling God to mind), and they say '*Waheguru*' (wonderful Lord) as the fingers touch each knot in turn.

Waheguru is the most popular name for God in Sikh devotion. Notice again that it is not the human or scriptural *guru* that it referred to, but God, the *Sat-Guru* (True Guru). He may also be called *Sat-Nam* (True Name) to distinguish him from the various named gods of Hinduism.

At a special moment in family life (when a new business is started, for example, or when there is some kind of trouble or someone has died) Sikhs may have a continuous reading of the *Guru Granth Sahib*. Various members of the family would take it in turns to read, and it takes about 48 hours to complete. This is called *Akhand Path*, and is performed in *gurdwaras* at all the main festivals. The end of this reading is called the *bhog* (conclusion) ceremony: the prayer *Ardas* is recited, and *Karah Parshad* is shared (see Chapter 8 for details of these).

From the *Guru Granth Sahib* there comes a distinctive way of life that Sikhs should follow, based on love through having God in mind (*simran*) and service to humanity (*seva*). All belief should show itself in practical action and, for a Sikh, belief in God is not enough to gain salvation, the follower must also show that faith in good deeds.

Service to humanity takes a threefold form:

1 **physical** *(Tan)* Sikhs are to engage in useful work. They should not rely on the charity of others. This is expressed also in the practical work of cooking and cleaning in the *gurdwara.*

2 **mental** *(Man)* Sikhs are required to study the Granth, to understand their religion and to be prepared to share it with others.

3 **material** *(Dhan)* 10% of all earnings is to be given to charity, which is distributed by the *gurdwara.*

Through spiritual discipline, the Sikh is to move through the *five khands,* which are five realms or levels of spiritual reality. They are taken from the *Japji:*

(1) *Dharam Khand* — the level of seeking moral duty
(2) *Gian Khand* — the level of wisdom and knowledge
(3) *Saram Khand* — the level of effort
(4) *Karam Khand* — the level of fulfilment
(5) *Sach Khand* — the level of truth, a state of permanent union with God

The aim of all this is to enable a person to overcome self-centredness, and to accept submission to God's Will. Only the person who is not grasping, but recognises that everything ultimately belongs to God, can be free to give and to love others.

The principles found in the *Granth* are straightforward and practical. The Sikh must remember to pray to God, must love and engage in honest work for the good of all. There is to be no caste distinction or sexual inequality: only actions decide who is good and who bad. The Sikh is therefore to be honest, simple in his or her food, dress and habits, and hospitable.

There is no merit in escaping from the world to seek holiness. There are no monks or celibate priesthood. Following the example of Nanak, all should be involved in work and family life. The idea of submitting to the Will of God is not defeatist in the face of suffering, but requires active participation to improve life and aid those who are oppressed.

Make sure you know
1 the full title of the Sikh scriptures
2 the most popular name for God
3 the threefold service required of a Sikh

See if you understand

4 why the *Granth* is called '*Guru*'
5 why a special room is needed for a copy of the Sikh scriptures
6 why there are no monks in Sikhism

Issues to discuss

7 Which are more important, your beliefs or your actions? On which would you rather be judged?

8 Gurdwaras

A sikh temple is called a *gurdwara*, which means '*guru's* door'. Strictly speaking, God himself is the true *guru*, so *gurdwara* could mean simply the place where one comes to meet God. But for Sikhs it is also the place where they present themselves before the *Guru Granth Sahib*. Indeed, any place where a copy of the *Guru Granth Sahib* is kept becomes a *gurdwara*. Originally, *gurdwaras* were called *dharmsalas*, resting places for travellers, where there would be the singing of hymns.

In Britain, most *gurdwaras* are buildings converted from some other use. They are distinguished by flying the Sikh flag:

Nishan Sahib

The two edged sword (*khanda*) represents the idea that Sikhs may be required to struggle with both physical and spiritual force. The two *kirpans* represent the spiritual and temporal authority of the *gurus*, and the circle expresses the unity of God. As an expression of the Sikh religion the flag is shown great respect, and worshippers may touch the flagpole before entering the *gurdwara*.

Also outside the *gurdwara* there may be a sign *ik oankar* meaning 'God is One'.

On entering the *gurdwara*, as a sign of respect, shoes are removed and heads are covered. Men wear their turbans and women cover their heads with a scarf which is normally draped over the shoulders.

Gurdwaras in the rural Punjab generally have washing facilities outside, and it is always required of a Sikh that he or she should bathe before attending the *gurdwara*. At the entrance, some Sikhs may stop on the steps and stoop down to touch them, lightly touching their forehead immediately afterwards. This tradition comes from the Indian way of showing respect to holy people by touching their feet. Because it contains the *Guru*, the *gurdwara* is a holy place, and touching the forehead with the dust from its steps signifies this, and expresses humility and modesty.

Inside the *gurdwara*, in the place of honour, raised up on a dais covered with a canopy and often enclosed within a wooden frame, is the *Guru Granth Sahib*. It may rest on a small bed, which looks like a low stool, or on a cushion. When not being read, it is covered with a silk cloth, called a *romalla*.

Originally the human *gurus* would have taught their followers from such an elevated position, and the *Guru Granth Sahib*, having now taken their place, is accorded the same respect. Behind it sits the reader (or *granthi*) who may wave over the scriptures a whisk of long animal hair, called a *chauri*. In the hot Indian climate, this would have kept away flies and offered the human *guru* some cooler fanned air. It is retained now as a sign of respect.

In the congregation (*sangat*) men and women sit on the floor. There are no raised seats, for all are to be equal and lower than the *Guru Granth Sahib* on its dais. As each worshipper enters, he or she approaches the sacred book and bows low, making an offering of food or money to be used by the *gurdwara* in the kitchens and for charitable purposes. Then they move back to sit down, with men on one side and women on the other, taking care never to turn their backs on the scriptures as they do so. Once there, they often sit cross-legged, as it is considered disrespectful to point one's feet towards the holy book.

Fig. 11   The people sit on the floor of the Gurdwara, men on one side and women on the other. Those standing have just arrived and are going forward to bow before the Guru Granth Sahib and make an offering. A garland is draped over the Granth as a sign of respect, and on the canopy over it the Sikh emblem is shown twice. Worship may start at 9.30 a.m. on a Sunday morning, and here (at 11.40 a.m by the clock) everything is still in full swing.

One member of the Sikh community is appointed to be the *granthi*, to read and expound the scriptures and to take care of the day to day running of the *gurdwara*. The *granthi* may be a man or a woman, and *any* Sikh who can read *Gurmukhi* fluently can act as *granthi* for the service. All are equal, and there is no ordained priesthood.

The Sikhs do not have a Sabbath or Holy Day, so they meet whenever it is most convenient. In Britain this is usually on a Sunday, although worship may go on throughout the week as individuals enter the *gurdwara* to spend a few moments before the *Guru Granth Sahib*. The service (or *diwan*) lasts several hours, and members of the congregation may come and go during that time. The atmosphere may seem quite informal.

The service is held for three reasons:

(1) to read and meditate upon the *Granth*
(2) to join in songs of praise
(3) to express and strengthen the unity and equality of the congregation.

This follows the pattern set down in 1521 when Guru Nanak settled at Kartapur.

There is no set order of worship. The *Guru Granth Sahib* may be opened at random, and a reading will be taken, starting from the top left hand page. This is called *hukam* (meaning 'the Will of God'), and may be followed by some words of explanation. It may take place at any point in the service, and after it the scriptures are again covered by the *romalla*.

The main feature of the service is the singing of portions of the *Guru Granth Sahib*. This is led by musicians (*ragis*) usually with a harmonium and drums. Since they do not have copies of the scriptures with them, members of the congregation will spend most of the time just listening, but may join in from time to time when they are familiar with the text. Usually, some explanation of the meaning of the chosen hymns will have been given (in Punjabi) before the singing, and the congregation can therefore reflect on their meaning.

As the service draws towards its close, there is a set order of events. While still seated, the congregation joins in two poems. The first is the *Anand Sahib*, or Hymn of Joy, composed by Guru Amar Das. It is a thanksgiving for the benefits of worship, and declares that all sorrow has now vanished. The second is the conclusion of the *Japji*. It says that man is made of the elements earth, water and air, and that one day all his deeds, good and bad, are to be judged by God. Worshippers pray that the faithful may receive joy and liberation.

Then all stand for the prayer. This is called *Ardas* (a word coming from the *sanskrit* root meaning 'to ask') and comes in three parts. First of all it recalls the human *gurus*, then it moves on to the original five members of the *Khalsa* and the martyrs of the Sikh community. Between verses the congregation respond by saying '*Waheguru!*' In the final section, the prayer asks that the worshippers should be freed from worldly attachment and vices, that they should receive the gifts of discernment and understanding of the scriptures, and that they should be forgiven for their faults. Special prayers are then added for any people in particular need, or about any situation of concern to the congregation. Finally, still standing with hands together, palms touching, the reader says 'The *Khalsa* is chosen of God' to which the congregation responds 'Victory belongs to God' — words used at the *Amrit* ceremony.

Then there is the final *Hukam* — the random reading of the scripture — believed to give the congregation some thought of special significance for that moment.

While all this has been going on, out in the kitchen, members of the congregation will have been preparing for the communal meal. (This may not take place after every act of worship, but is usual on Sundays and all festivals.) But one special type of food will always have been prepared and brought into the *gurdwara*, to stand next to the *Guru Granth Sahib* and to be blessed by the final prayers and reading. This is called *Karah Parshad*.

Having taken a bath (to express purity of mind as well as body), and while reciting hymns, a Sikh prepares the *karah parshad* at the beginning of the service. It is a mixture of equal parts of sugar, water, butter and semolina (or plain flour); sweet and dough-like. During the final prayers, a *kirpan* is held up before this food, and is then used to touch or stir it as a sign of blessing.

One small portion is offered to the *Guru Granth Sahib*, and five others are taken to represent the first five members of the *Khalsa*, and given to any five baptised Sikhs present. The remainder is then distributed to the congregation, including visitors of other faiths. Its sweetness represents the kindness of God, and its sharing is a sign that everyone is treated equally and that no one is sent away from worship hungry.

Guru Nanak had a communal kitchen at Kartarpur, and Guru Amar Das ordered that every *gurdwara* should have one. All Sikhs should overcome their caste differences by sitting and eating together. This kitchen is called the *langar*. The food served in it is vegetarian. This is because, although there are no strict food laws for Sikhs, it is important not to give offence to those who will not eat meat. Many Sikhs prefer to be vegetarian rather than to do violence to animal life. The meal is taken sitting or standing (it does not matter which, as long as everyone does the same) and is traditionally eaten with the right hand. This is made easier because the meal will usually include *chapattis* (flat, pancake-like bread) which can be dipped into sauces or used to scoop up vegetables.

At the end of the day, the *granthi* says the prayer *Ardas* and has a final reading from the *Guru Granth Sahib*. He then covers his head with a clean cloth, wraps the scriptures in another one and then puts the

41

romalla back over it. The scriptures are then carried out of the *gurdwara* by a bearer who places it on his head (his turban having first been covered with a cloth) so that it is always held *above* those present, who stand silently as it is taken out. At night the *Guru Granth Sahib* rests on a bed under a canopy — always treated with the respect that would be shown to one of the human *gurus*. Where there is no separate room, the scriptures stay in the *gurdwara*, and are covered by a *romalla*.

During the week, *gurdwaras* may be open so that Sikhs can enter and spend a few moments before the *Guru Granth Sahib*. It is also a community centre, and there may be classes in Punjabi and Sikh religious thought. This is especially important for Sikhs living far from the Punjab, and strengthens their sense of identity.

In India, many *gurdwaras* will offer a bed for the night to travellers, and the *langar* will be the means of dispensing charity. Many *gurdwaras* there also serve as health clinics.

These social functions are not an optional extra for *gurdwaras*. Although their main task is to house the *Guru Granth Sahib*, the Sikh religion requires that belief finds expression in practical activity, and the *gurdwara* shows that by its social and charitable work.

Make sure you know
1 the meaning of the word *gurdwara*
2 at least three ways in which respect is shown to the *Guru Granth Sahib* in the *gurdwara*

See if you understand
3 why the *Guru Granth Sahib* is always raised up above the level of the people
4 why food is shared at the end of the service in the *langar*

Issues to discuss
5 The word *Hukam* can refer to the Will of God, ordering and organising the world. It is also used for the chance reading from the *Granth*, which is used for guidance, taking whatever verses come to hand when the scriptures are opened. How might these two things be related to one another?
6 Is it better to have a fixed order of service, or the less formal Sikh approach?

9 Birth, marriage and death

Birth

A few weeks after the birth of a child, mother and baby go to the *gurdwara*, taking with them the ingredients for making *karah parshad*. It is also customary to make a gift of an embroidered *romalla*.

The family gather round, and while verses of the *Japji* are being read, the *granthi* mixes together the sugar and water for *amrit* in a bowl. He stirs it with a two edged sword (*khanda*). The prayer *Ardas* is said (as at all acts of worship), and concludes with special prayers for the child, that he or she may grow up to be a true Sikh. Then the *granthi* dips the tip of his *kirpan* into the *amrit*, and puts it to the child's lips. The remainder is then drunk by the mother.

Then the *Guru Granth Sahib* is opened at random and the first letter of the first word of the hymn on the left hand page is noted. The parents choose a name for their child starting with that letter, and it is announced to the congregation. After that, all share the *karah parshad*.

Many Sikh names can be given to either a boy or a girl, and it is necessary to add *Singh* (for a boy) and *Kaur* (for a girl) in order to distinguish between them. Strictly speaking, these titles are used only after the *Amrit* ceremony (see Chapter 6) but in practice they are used before it, or by Sikhs who have not been through initiation.

Because of the confusion caused by having so many people called either *Singh* or *Kaur*, surnames are still used. Traditionally, they were abolished by the *Khalsa* in order to get rid of caste distinctions. The correct title to use when speaking of Sikh men and women is *Sardar* (Mr) and *Sardarni* (Mrs). If you do not know a man's name, the polite thing to do is to call him *Sardarji*, which is the equivalent of the English term 'Sir'.

The naming of a child is a time for family celebrations. Presents are exchanged, and gifts are also made to charity.

Marriage

In the Sikh religion men and women are equal, and all Sikhs are required to take marriage and family responsibilities seriously. It is usual for the choice of a marriage partner to be made by the whole family rather than by the boy or girl concerned. The reasons given for this are that in India the extended family still tends to live together. A new bride will need to get on with her in-laws as well as her husband. It is also thought that the experience of the older married members of the family will be important in selecting a suitable partner. This is usually called 'assisted' marriage rather than 'arranged' marriage, for the couple are given the opportunity to express their own views about the proposed match, and can decline the person selected by their family.

Sometimes, particularly in the West, Sikhs do choose their own partners. In this case it is usual to discuss the matter with the family, who will then go through the usual process, as though the choice had been theirs. There does not seem to be any evidence that marriages assisted in this way are any less happy than the love matches of western culture.

The families enquire very carefully about the health, disposition and educational qualifications of the suggested partners. If they are satisfied, the couple are encouraged to meet and get to know one another — although they may not do this in private, but only in the company of other members of the family. Once everything is decided, the parents of the bride go to the prospective groom's house and present him with gifts, often including a *kirpan*. The girl will not be present when this happens, but may also receive gifts at this time.

The wedding itself is called *Anand Karaj* (Ceremony of Bliss). The men from the families meet early in the *gurdwara*, exchange gifts — traditionally turbans — and take refreshments together.

Bride and groom sit in front of the *Guru Granth Sahib*. She will wear a red scarf (*dupatta*), red or pink trousers (*shalwar*) and a gold embroidered tunic (*kameeze*). He will usually wear a red or pink turban. The *granthi* expounds on the Sikh understanding of marriage. Sexual union is regarded as a special and sacred moment in which men and women share in the creative work of God, and they are to grow spiritually through their love for one another. The bride and groom bow to show that they accept the responsibilities of marriage, and the bride's father places a garland upon the *Guru Granth Sahib*, and then others round the necks of the couple.

The bride's father then ties the bride and groom together. He takes the groom's saffron coloured scarf, passes it over his shoulder and then puts it into the hand of the bride. Thus locked together, they listen while the *granthi* reads out the four verses of the *Lavan*, or wedding hymn, composed for his daughter's wedding by Guru Ram Das (*Granth* page 773). The verses speak of the stages of love, and expresses the union of the self with God — a union which is to be mirrored in the love of husband and wife.

As each verse is completed, bride and groom bow to show that they accept it, and then stand and walk in a clockwise direction round the *Guru Granth Sahib*. While they do this, the musicians sing that same verse of the *Lavan*. After the fourth verse, as they walk round, the congregation shower them with flower petals.

Fig. 12   A Sikh Wedding. The bride holds the end of the groom's scarf, a sign that they are joined together. They sit before a copy of the Granth, surrounded by family and friends.

The service ends in the usual way — with the prayer *Ardas*, the *hukam* or chance reading from the *Guru Granth Sahib*, and the sharing of *karah parshad*. Since this ceremony has taken place in front of the *Guru Granth Sahib*, there is no need for the couple to sign any documents. The scriptures are the only witness necessary. In Britain it will be necessary for the marriage to be registered by a civil registrar, but this is not part of the Sikh marriage itself.

Celebrations may start at the *gurdwara*, and the wedding party then go first to the bride's house. Here she says 'goodbye' officially to her family, and is then taken by the groom to his family, where she is to make her new home.

Once married, divorce is rare, and is against the principles of the Sikh religion. In the case of separation, the wife usually returns to her family home.

Although the service emphasises that a wife should strive to serve and please her husband, the status of women in Sikhism is high. Wives are traditionally called *ardhangi* (meaning 'better half') and the *Guru Granth Sahib* says many positive things about the role of women in friendship, childbearing and the establishment of a home and of society.

Compared with the Hinduism of the time, Sikhism made major advances towards sex equality. Guru Amar Das ruled that *suttee* (the practice of burning widows on their husband's funeral pyre) should not be allowed. Although widows do not usually remarry, they are treated with respect within the community, whereas within the Hindu culture they were traditionally regarded as bringers of bad luck, and therefore shunned.

It should be remembered that the shyness and retiring nature of some Sikh women in public does not indicate that they have an inferior status. It is just that modesty is regarded as a quality to be valued.

Death

Guru Nanak died at Kartarpur, and there is a tradition that, as he was dying, there was a debate among his followers. The Muslims wanted his body to be buried; the Hindus wanted it cremated. Guru Nanak told them to place flowers on either side of him, one bunch representing each of the religious groups. Whichever bunch was still fresh in the morning, that group should have charge over his funeral arrangements. Then he covered himself over and slept. Next morning they came to him but found that his body had vanished, but that both bunches of flowers had bloomed!

When a Sikh dies, the body is washed and dressed and put in a coffin with the five 'K's to signify membership of the *Khalsa*. The adult relatives may then take part in the continuous reading of the *Guru Granth Sahib* for the next forty-eight hours or so. The body is then cremated.

In Britain there is usually a service in the *gurdwara* (although the coffin is not brought into the presence of the *Guru Granth Sahib*, but left in another room), followed by cremation at a crematorium. Memorials are not allowed and a deliberate show of grief is forbidden.

Sikhs believe that there is a part of God in each person, which will finally be reunited with him. The soul is therefore immortal. The final bliss of union with God is believed to be brought about partly by the good works that a person performs and partly by the grace of God. Until that time, the soul may need to be reborn, until it is ready for that union with God. Nevertheless, the Sikh always hopes that the person who has died has already been liberated into God, and does not regard the death of someone as a time of sadness.

The Sikh attitude to death is summed up in the following poem by Guru Gobind Singh:

As myriads of sparks rise from one fire
And go apart in various directions,
But ultimately come back to merge in the same earth;
As myriads of particles rise from the earth, and go apart;
But ultimately come back to merge in the same earth;
As myriads of waves arise from the same ocean,
But ultimately come back to merge in the same water;
So do myriads of forms, sentient and insentient,
Rise from the same vast form of God,
And ultimately come back to Him.

A hymn that is sometimes sung just before cremation is by the Hindu poet Ravidas:

The dawn of a new day
Is the herald of a sunset,
Earth is not thy permanent home.
Life is like a shadow on a wall.

Close relatives say prayers for the dead person in the *gurdwara* or at home for a period of ten days after the death. The final prayer that is said before the cremation itself is the one that Sikhs repeat before bed every night.

Make sure you know
1 how a child's name is chosen
2 the action that bride and groom perform during the wedding ceremony
3 how Sikhs dispose of the body of a dead person

See if you understand
4 how the idea of the 'extended family' has influenced Sikh marriage and the choice of a marriage partner

5   what Sikhs feel about death, and how it relates to their idea of God

Issues to discuss
6   Is it right for families to decide whom you should marry?
7   Is it a good idea to discourage a public show of grief at funerals?

10 Festivals

There are two kinds of festivals celebrated by Sikhs, *Melas* and *Gurpurbs*.

The *melas* are Sikh celebrations and fairs. As the young Sikh community developed, it became important to distinguish Sikhs from among the Hindu population. Guru Amar Das therefore ordered that they should gather together three times a year at the same time as the Hindus were having their own festivals. They did this at Goindwal, where the Guru built an artificial lake with steps for bathing, following Hindu custom at holy places. It became a religious centre for Sikhs.

There are three main *melas* celebrated today, *Baisakhi, Diwali* and *Hola Mohalla.*

Baisakhi

This is celebrated on April 13th, and is the Sikh New Year. Although it takes place while Hindus are celebrating their Spring festival, it has a special meaning for Sikhs, for at *Baisakhi* 1699 Guru Gobind Singh started the *Khalsa* (see Chapter 6). It therefore represents the birthday of Sikhism as we know it today. It is a time when young Sikhs are baptised at the *Amrit Pahul* (initiation) ceremony and take on the full responsibilities as members of the *Khalsa.*

In the 18th century, the separate Sikh groups (called '*misls*') used to meet together in Amritsar for *Baisakhi*, and there made decisions about the life of the whole Sikh community, following the principle of *guru panth* (see Chapter 7). A similar thing happens today, for *Baisakhi* is the time when each Sikh community meets to elect the committee which will run their *gurdwara* for the coming year.

For Sikhs, like Hindus, *Baisakhi* is a spring festival. Many visit Amritsar, going to the Golden Temple and bathing in the holy lake. During the afternoon, in a place called Jallianwala Bagh, there are political rallies, and outside the city there is an animal fair. Throughout the Punjab, it is a time of rest before the work of harvesting.

Diwali

This is celebrated during October or November (following the Hindu lunar calendar), and has some features in common with the Hindu festival of the same name. In Hinduism, it is a time to celebrate the victorious return of Prince Rama and his loyal wife Sita after she has been saved from the hands of the demon king Ravana — following the story in the *Ramayana* epic. It recalls the victory of good over evil, and houses and temples are lit by rows of lamps.

Diwali in Amritsar uses the same symbol of light. There are firework displays, and the Golden Temple is lit by hundreds of lamps. The Sikhs recall a particular moment in their history. Guru Hargobind had been held in the fortress of Gwalior by the Emperor Jehangir, under suspicion of treachery. The charges against him were examined, and he was found to be innocent. When his release was announced, he agreed to leave only if he could take with him the 52 princes with whom he had shared his prison. The Emperor agreed to this on one condition. Only those could leave who could cling to the coat of the *guru* as they did so. Tradition records that Hargobind sent for a coat with long tassels hanging from it and, clinging to them, all the Hindu princes were saved. It is therefore a time to celebrate freedom from oppression.

Hola Mohalla

This festival was started by Guru Gobind Singh in 1680, to take place at the time of the Hindu *Holi* celebrations. Originally it was a time of military exercises and training, and it still has something of that character. Today it is celebrated mainly around Anandpur, in the Punjab, and consists of three days of competitions, especially horseriding and athletics. It is also a celebration of the arts, music and poetry. It takes place in February or March.

The festivals can be celebrated anywhere, and there is no religious obligation to go on pilgrimage in Sikhism. Of course, certain special events — such as *Diwali* at Amritsar or *Hola Mohulla* at Anandpur — will attract Sikhs from far afield, but the essence of pilgrimage for a Sikh is the *inner* journey. A pious Sikh can therefore make any journey a pilgrimage, or can go on a spiritual pilgrimage without travelling at all.

Gurpurbs

'*Purb*' means 'holiday'. Therefore *gurpurbs* are holidays associated with the *gurus*. Four of these are widely observed: the birthdays of Guru Nanak and Guru Gobind Singh, and the martyrdoms of Guru Arjan and Guru Tegh Bahadur. This last *gurpurb* is celebrated especially in Delhi, where he was killed, and many other *gurpurbs* are celebrated only in the particular place associated with the historical event that the *gurpurb* recalls.

The main celebrations will take place on the Sunday after the actual anniversary, in order that the maximum number of Sikhs can take part. There are two features of the worship which distinguish the *gurpurb* from the ordinary weekly meeting. The first is that for forty-eight hours leading up to the Sunday morning *diwan* there is a continuous reading of the *Guru Granth Sahib*. The second is that on the Sunday

Fig. 13   On festivals the Guru Granth Sahib may be carried through the streets in procession. Here it is in an elaborately decorated carriage as it passes through the streets of Delhi.

morning (and the two preceding days) there is a meal in the *langar*.

For the birthday of Guru Nanak — the most important of the *gurpurbs* as far as celebrations go — the festivities last for three days, and (where possible) the *Guru Granth Sahib* is carried in procession behind five men who represent the first five members of the *Khalsa*.

The calendar for Sikhs will therefore contain the following festivals:

April 13th	*Baisakhi Mela*
May/June	Martyrdom of Guru Arjan
October/November	*Diwali Mela*
	Birthday of Guru Nanak
December	Martyrdom of Guru Tegh Bahadur
	Birthday of Guru Gobind Singh
February/March	*Hola Mohalla Mela*

With the exception of the New Year on April 13th, the festivals follow the Hindu lunar calendar and do not therefore fall regularly on the same day in our western Gregorian calendar.

You may notice that Guru Nanak has two birthdays! In Chapter 2 it was said to be April 15th, and this follows the majority of the *Janam Sakhis*. But the influential *Bala Janam Sakhi* has a November date, and it is this that is celebrated.

Make sure you know
1   the names of the three main festivals
2   the meaning of the word '*gurpurb*'

See if you understand
3   why Sikhs hold some festivals at the same time as Hindus
4   why there is no tradition of pilgrimage in Sikhism

Issues to discuss
5   For both Hindus and Sikhs, light is used for the celebration of *Diwali*. Of what is it symbolic, and why is it an appropriate symbol for those festivals?
6   Is it necessary for a religion or culture to celebrate particular days of the year?

11 The Sikhs today

The majority of Sikhs still live in the Indian state of Punjab, where, led by the Akali Dal party, many have been demanding greater autonomy for the Sikh community. Others were prepared to use violent means to establish an independent Sikh nation, to be called Khalistan ('Land of the Pure'), and led by Sant Jarnail Singh Bhindranwale they armed themselves and established a headquarters in the Golden Temple at Amritsar. After months of demonstrations, riots and killings, the Indian army attacked the Golden Temple in June 1984, killing Bhindranwale and many of his followers. This military action was greatly resented by the Sikh community, who continue to press for political change in the Punjab.

To see why this happened, we need to look at the history of the Sikh community since the death of Guru Gobind Singh in 1708.

For some years, Banda Singh, his military commander, was successful, and sought to establish a Sikh government. But in 1716 he was defeated, captured and, with his son and several thousand followers, killed with extreme barbarity. The Sikh religion was then outlawed.

From then until 1765 there followed years of bloodshed, with attempts to establish political control, followed by ruthless persecution. Finally, a commonwealth of the *Khalsa* was set up, with its Council at Amritsar, to which representatives of the twelve separate *Khalsa* groups who were ruling different parts of the country could gather to discuss matters of national importance.

Eventually the confederacy of these groups was abolished, and power came into the hands of Maharaja Rangit Singh, who captured Lahore in 1799 and made it his capital. He ruled an independent Sikh state for forty years, until his death in 1839. He was greatly loved by Sikhs, and in that time of peace Guru Arjan's Harimandir was rebuilt and decorated as it is today, and many other *gurdwaras* were established. His rule is regarded by many as an ideal to which they would wish to return. It was almost the only time of peace in the Punjab since the establishment of the Sikh religion.

Following his death, further trouble broke out. Since 1809 there had been a treaty of friendship with the British, who by that time ruled most of India, but provoked by the British and encouraged by internal struggles, fighting broke out, and in 1846 the British Army arrived at

Lahore. Tribute was paid, and the Sikh army disbanded. In 1851 the young Maharaja Dalip Singh was accused of rebellion and exiled to Britain; his kingdom was then annexed to the British Empire. There he campaigned for the return of the Kon-i-noor diamond, which had been presented to Queen Victoria by Maharaja Ranjit Singh, and for the restoration of his kingdom. His wishes were not fulfilled, and he died in Paris in 1893.

So after their brief time of independence, the Sikhs lived under British rule, and remained loyal to the British during the Indian Mutiny of 1857. Many served in the army and police force: being neither Muslim nor Hindu they could be relied on for impartiality. Others struggled to maintain Sikh cultural and political independence. They insisted on the right to assemble for their festivals, and to control their *gurdwaras*.

In 1919, Sikhs assembled for *Baisakhi* in the Jallianwala Bagh in Amritsar as usual, in spite of the British order forbidding political meetings. General Dyer brought in troops and fired into the assembly, killing three hundred and thirty-seven men, forty-one boys and a baby, and wounding many more. It was a moment that hardened the Sikh determination to achieve independence.

The following year the Akali Dal party was formed, to take over the running of the *gurdwaras*, and after many were killed and thousands arrested, the Sikh Gurdwaras Act of 1925 allowed Sikhs the control they sought.

With the partition of India in 1947, terrible rioting broke out in the Punjab. At that time there were about 15 million Hindus, 16 million Muslims and 6 million Sikhs living there. The division between India and Pakistan was made through the Punjab, leaving 80% of the Sikhs on the Pakistan side — the area reserved for Muslims. In the exodus that followed it is estimated that about half a million Sikhs died, and 11½ million Sikhs and Hindus were made refugees. On the Indian side of the line, the new state of Punjab was only one third of the original area of the Punjab, and could not support its new population.

In 1966 the state of Punjab, with its capital at Chandigarh, was divided into two parts. The north became Punjab, with a majority of Sikhs, Punjabi as the official language and the Gurmukhi script. The south, with a Hindu majority, became the state of Haryana.

From the 19th century there sprang up two reform movements within Sikhism. The Nirankaris were strictly against idolatry, and wanted to strip the *gurdwaras* of all Hindu practices. They also rejected the need for the initiation into the *Khalsa*. Sometimes called Nanak *panthis*, their influence has now diminished. The other movement is that of the Namdharis. Strictly vegetarian and taking violent action against those who sold meat, they were outlawed and became peripheral to Sikhism. They believe that there were a succession of human *gurus* after Guru Gobind Singh. The present *guru*, Jagit Singh, regards himself

Fig. 14   Sikhs are allowed to wear turbans instead of crash helmets
in Britain — a concession which was won only after a long legal struggle.
The turban is an important sign of belonging to the Sikh community.

as vicegerent, standing in for Guru Ram Singh, who was made Guru in 1861 and who, after disappearing, is expected to return. There are about 700,000 Namdharis. They do not give absolute authority to the *Guru Granth Sahib*, and call their places of worship *dharmsalas* rather than *gurdwaras*.

Sikhs have emigrated to Britain since the early 1950's, and many of them have come from one particular area of the Punjab around the city of Jullundur. Although some have become westernised in their dress and have cut their hair and beards, there remains a strong sense of Sikh identity with men wearing turbans and women the *shalwar* and *kameeze*. There are over 50 *gurdwaras* in this country. The major Sikh communities are to be found in the London area in Southall, Woolwich and Gravesend, around Birmingham, and in the East Midlands. Their openness towards those of other religions, and the adaptability of their religious festivals to suit the British tradition of worship on Sundays, has helped them to blend into British society. One exception to this has been the dispute over the wearing of turbans rather than crash helmets when riding motorcycles. After years of protest, the Sikhs won this concession.

Sikhism is a way of devotion and a pattern of life. It is not a religion that has attempted to set down beliefs that must be accepted literally by all its members. In particular, it does *not* require belief in supernatural activities — e.g. miracles. This has saved the Sikh faith from a confrontation within modern science. The *Guru Granth Sahib* accepts that there may be worlds beyond our own, and that we cannot know everything about the universe. God is described primarily as a spirit encountered within the self, a light that can shine out to illuminate the world. It does not depend for its beliefs on any one particular philosophy about the nature of the world or God's place within it. This makes all modern scientific theories about the universe compatible with the Sikh religion.

Only time will tell how the Sikh faith may become changed within the communities that are far removed from the Punjab homeland. Yet being a Sikh is only superficially a matter of wearing a certain sort of dress that originated in that part of India. What is far more important now (and has been ever since the death of Guru Gobind Singh) is the presence of the *Guru Granth Sahib*. Wherever it is kept, there is the *gurdwara*, and there is the place for all the major events of life — it names a young child and certifies a marriage; before it a young Sikh receives his baptism; and it is read through by the mourners when a Sikh has died. Sikhism is a religion based on its sacred scriptures. It may therefore retain its language, customs and ceremonies, even if the culture in which it finds itself changes drastically.

Anyone, of any race, who is prepared to accept belief in one God, in the teachings of the ten *gurus* and of the *Guru Granth Sahib*, and to submit to *Amrit* baptism, can become a Sikh. Therefore, although numerically small, Sikhism is a world religion.

Make sure you know
1 the name of the 19th century ruler of the independent Sikh kingdom
2 the date of the partition of India and the names of the countries into which it was divided

See if you understand
3 why the Punjab has seen such violence in modern times
4 why Sikhism is not threatened by modern science

Issues to discuss
5 Is it right for a religion to influence politics?
6 Is it better to have a religion based on a present day human teacher (or teachers) or on religious writings from the past?

Word list

Adi Sri Guru Granth Sahib	Sikh scripture
akal	eternal
Akal Takht	chief seat of religious authority, Amritsar
Akali Dal	Sikh political party
Akhand Path	continuous reading of the scripture
Amrit (or Amrit Pahul)	the Sikh initiation ceremony (the term Amrit refers to the sweetened water used)
anami	beyond names (used of God)
Anand Keraj	ceremony of bliss, a wedding
Anand Sahib	'Song of Joy' from the Granth
Ardas	Sikh common prayer
ardhangi	Sikh term for wife (it means 'better half')
Baisakhi	Sikh New Year Festival
Bala Janam Sakhi	a popular set of birth stories, incorporating material on Bala
Bhakti	a Hindu devotional tradition
Bhog	the ceremony that ends the continuous reading of the Granth
chapatti	flat Indian bread
chauri	a fan of animal hair, waved over the Granth as a sign of its authority
chunni (or dupatta)	a scarf worn by Sikh women
darsan	private time before the Guru Granth Sahib
Dasam Granth	the collection of writings of Guru Gobind Singh
dhan	material; one of the three forms of service (*seva*)
dharmsalas	resting places for travellers, an early term for Gurdwaras
dhoti	traditional Hindu garment
Diwali	Sikh festival
diwan	act of worship
Granth	'writing'; shortened name for the scriptures
gurdwara	Sikh temple
Gurmat	the guru's teaching; Sikh doctrine
Gurmukh	a person who reveals the guru's voice
Gurmukhi	the script used for Punjabi
gurpurbs	anniversaries of the birth or death of gurus
guru	teacher

Guru Panth	doctrine (especially in the 18th century) of the inspiration of the community
gutka	selection of the scriptures
Hatha Yoga	spiritual discipline involving physical actions
Hola Mohalla	Sikh festival
Hukam	order (God's will for the universe); also used for a chance reading of the scriptures
ik oankar	'God is One', sometimes written up outside a gurdwara
Janam Sakhis	birth evidences; stories about Guru Nanak
Japji	the opening section of the Granth
Kachha	shorts
Kameeze	form of dress worn by Sikh women
Kangha	comb
Kara	bangle
Karah Parshad	sweet food eaten at the end of worship
Karma	law that binds creatures to the cycle of reincarnation
Kaur	'princess'; term used for women members of the Khalsa
Kesh	hair
Kesh Dhari Singh	a baptised Sikh; a member of the Khalsa
Khanda	the double edged sword
Khands (the Five)	stages of spiritual development in the Japji
Kirpan	sword
langar	communal kitchen
Lavan	the wedding hymn
mala	cotton rosary of 108 knots
man	'mind'; one of the forms of service
manmukh	a person who displays only his own mind and self-interest
maya	illusion
mela	festival
misls	groups who ruled the Sikh community in the 18th century
Mool Mantra	first passage in the Granth; basic statement of faith
Mukti (Hindu: Moksha)	release; salvation
Nam	'name', used of God
Nam Simran	keeping God's name in mind
Namdharis	19th century reform movement
Nath	a tradition of interior discipline in Hinduism
Nirankaris	a reform movement in Sikhism
non-karmic birth	a birth (e.g. of the gurus) not required by Karma, but chosen for the purpose of bringing religious salvation
Pangat	'row' of people eating together
pauri	stanza (of the Japji)
ragis	musicians (also, *rag* – tune; used as a division in the Granth)
rebec	stringed instrument

romalla	cloth covering the Granth
Sabad	word; hymn
Sanskrit	Hindu sacred language
Sangat	congregation; used of the Sikh community
Sant	devotional tradition in Hinduism (a branch of *Bhakti*)
Sahaj Dhari	a non-amrit Sikh
Sat	true (used of God)
Sat Guru	true guru (of God): also *Sat Nam*, True Name
Seva	service: moral and practical obligations of a Sikh
shalwar	baggy trousers worn by Sikh women
Simran	shortened term for *Nam Simran*, keeping God in mind
Singh	'lion' used of a baptised Sikh male
suttee	burning a widow on her husband's funeral pyre
tan	'physical'; one of the forms of service
turban	length of cloth wrapped round the head, enclosing the hair
udasis	a term used for Guru Nanak's missions
Waheguru	popular term for God

Useful addresses:-

The Sikh Cultural Centre,
88 Mollison Way, Edgware, Middlesex HA8 5QW
This centre is able to give information about gurdwaras and other Sikh organisations. At the same address may be found the offices of *The Sikh Courier,* a quarterly journal.

Index

Adi Granth (*see* Guru Granth
   Sahib)
Akal Takht 32
Akali Dal 53
Akbar 22
Akhand Path 34
Amar Das (Guru) 20
Amrit Dhari 29
Amrit Sanskar 26, 28, 29, 41, 57
Amritsar 1, 22, 24, 26, 32, 40, 50,
   53
Anand Karaj 44
Anand Sahib 40
Angad (Guru) 20
Anandpur 25, 32, 50
Ardas 34, 40, 41, 43, 46
Ardhangi 46
Arjan (Guru) 20ff, 50, 52
Aurangzeb 25

Baisakhi 25, 49, 54
Bala 4
Banda Singh 31, 53
Beas (River) 1
Bhai Diala 25
Bhai Gurdas 7
Bhai Mati Das 25
Bhindranwale 53
British Army 53f
Buddha 13

Chamkaur (Battle) 31
Chapattis 41
Chauri 38
Chenab (River) 1

Dalip Singh 54
Dasam Granth 31, 34

Dharmsala 37, 56
Diwali 49, 50, 52
Diwan 40
Dupatta 3, 44

Gobind Singh (Guru) 20, 24, 25ff,
   32, 47, 50, 52, 53
Granthi 40, 44
Gurdwara 22, 32, 34, 37ff, 43,
   46, 47, 49, 54
Gurmat 7
Gurmukh 7
Gurmukhi (Script) 9, 20f, 40, 54
Gurpurbs 54
Guru 1, 7, 20ff, 26, 32, 34,
   37f, 50, 56
Guru Granth Sahib 3, 7, 29, 32ff,
   34, 38, 41f, 44, 46f, 50f, 56
Gutka 34
Gwalior 22, 50

Har Krishan (Guru) 20, 25
Har Rai (Guru) 20, 25
Hargobind (Guru) 20, 22, 50
Harimandir (Golden Temple;
   Darbar Sahib) 22, 53
Haryana 54
Hindu (Hinduism) 1, 5, 9ff, 16,
   46, 47, 49f, 54
Hola Mohalla 50
Hukam 16, 18, 40f, 46

Ik Oankar 38
Islam (Muslim) 1, 5, 9ff, 46, 54

Jallianwala Bagh 49, 54
Janam Sakhis 4, 14, 52

Jangit Singh 54
Japji 17f, 21, 35, 40
Jats 24, 31
Jehangir 22, 50
Jehlam (River) 1
Jesus 13
Jullundur 56

Ka'aba 14
Kabir 5, 21
Kachha 26
Kameeze 3, 44, 56
Kangha 29
Kara 27
Karah Parshad 41, 43, 46
Karma 5
Kartarpur 7, 21, 46
Kashmir 25
Kesh 28
Kesh Dhari Singh 26
Khalistan 53
Khalsa 25, 26, 28f, 31f, 42, 43, 46, 51, 53f
Khanda 29, 37
Khands 35
Kirpan 28f, 37, 41, 44
Kshatriya Caste 24

Lahore 22, 24, 53
Langar 7, 41
Lavan 44

Mahala 21
Mala 6
Manmukh 7
Mardana 4, 7, 14
Maya 16
Mecca 7
Mela 49ff
Moksha 12
Mool Mantra 12, 14, 17, 21
Moses 13
Mughal Empire 22, 25
Muhammad 13
Mukti 16

Nam 16, 17f
Nam Simran 34
Namdharis 54, 56

Nanak 1, 4ff, 20f, 24, 34, 40, 46, 50ff
Nanded 32
Nirankaris 43
Nishan Sahib 37
Non-karmic birth 13

Pakistan 54
Pangat 7
Panj Piares 26
Panth 9
Patna Sahib 32
Pauri 18
Punjab 1, 53, 54

Rag 21
Ragis 40
Ram Das (Guru) 20f, 44
Ram Singh (Guru) 56
Ramayana Epic 50
Ranjit Singh 1, 24, 53f
Ravi (River) 1, 22
Ravidas 47
Rebec 7
Rehat Maryada 31
Romalla 38, 40, 42

Sabad 16
Sahaj Dhari 26
Sakti 24
Sangat 7, 38
Sant 5
Sardar/Sardani/Sardarji 43
Sat Guru 34
Sat Nam 16, 34
Seva 34
Shalwar 3, 44, 56
Shivalik Hills 22, 24
Singh 26, 43
Sirhind 31
Sulakhani 4
Sutlej (River) 1
Suttee 46

Takht 32
Tegh Bahadur (Guru) 14, 20, 25, 50, 52
Turban 28, 44

Waheguru 34, 40